Welcome to Women of Japan Coloring Book

By: AH64Designs

Inside you will find 20 full pages of beautiful Japanese style women coloring art. Never stop having fun.

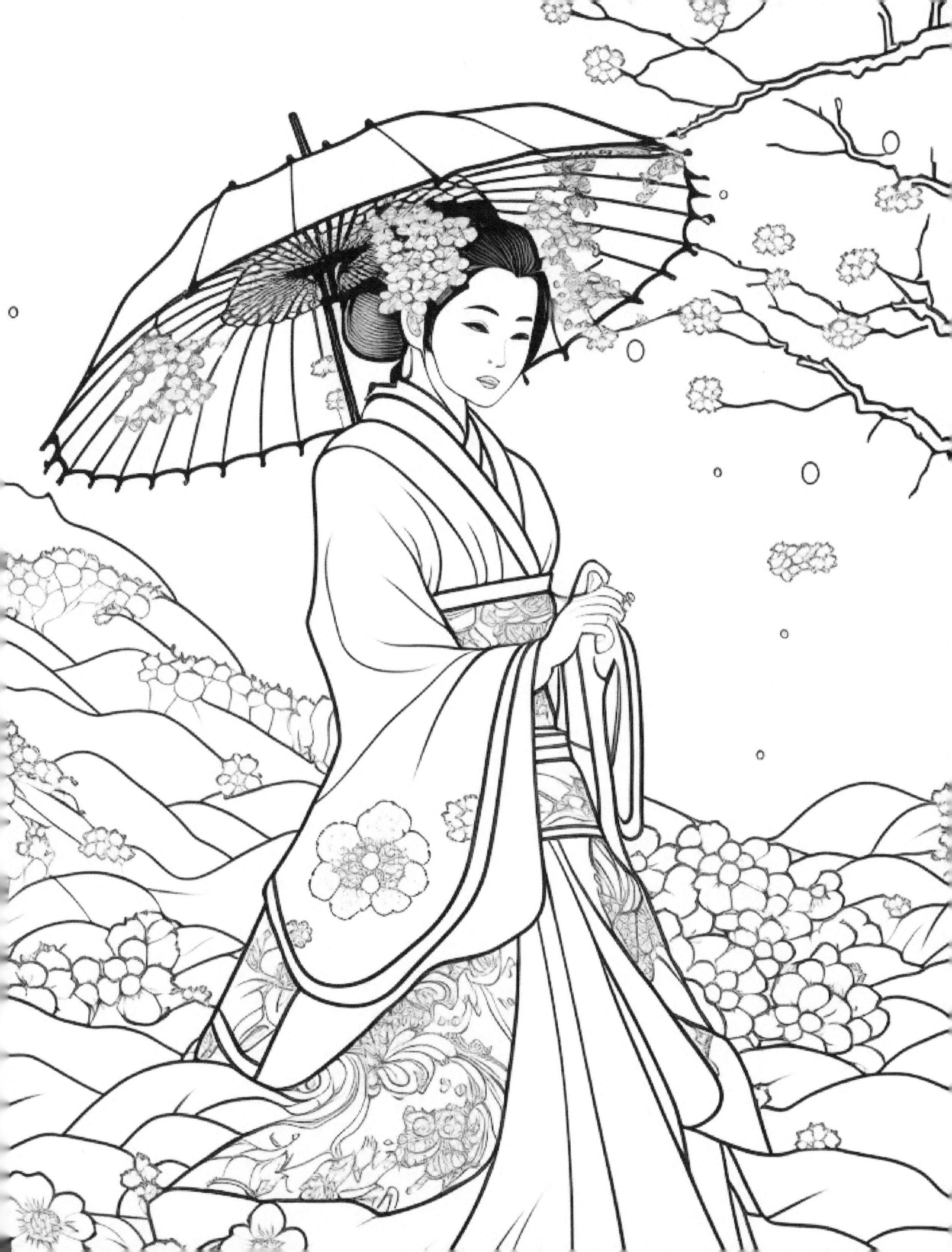

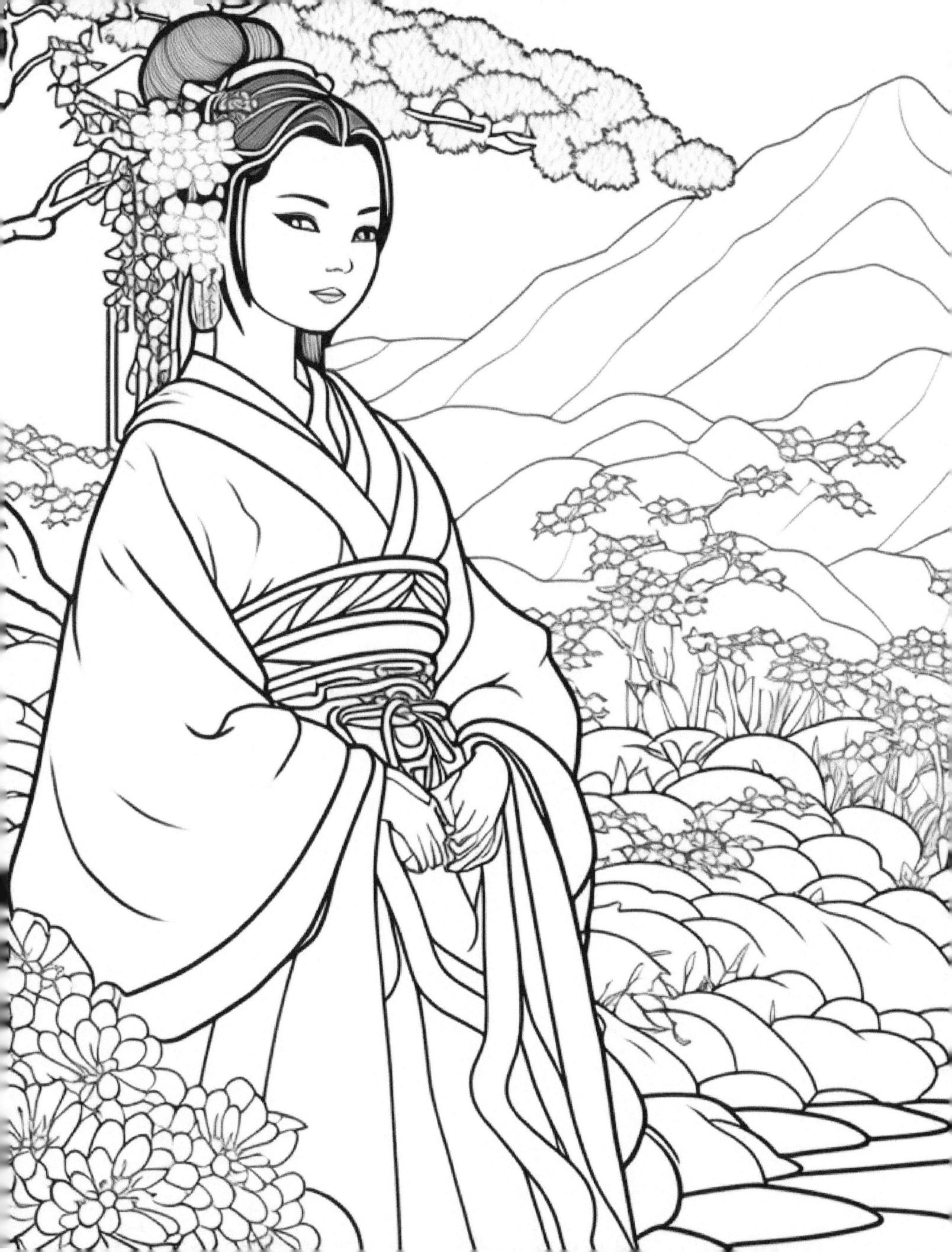

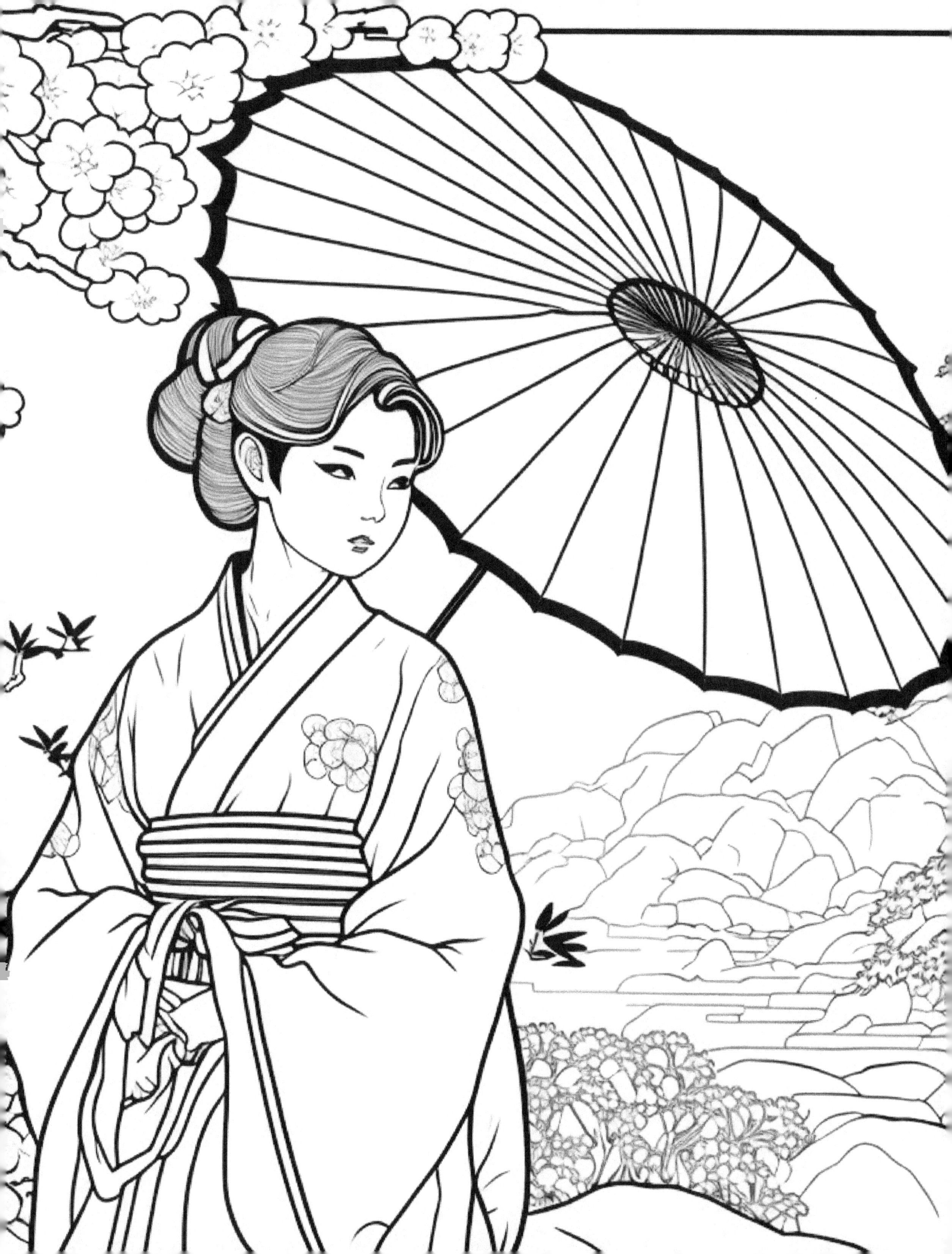

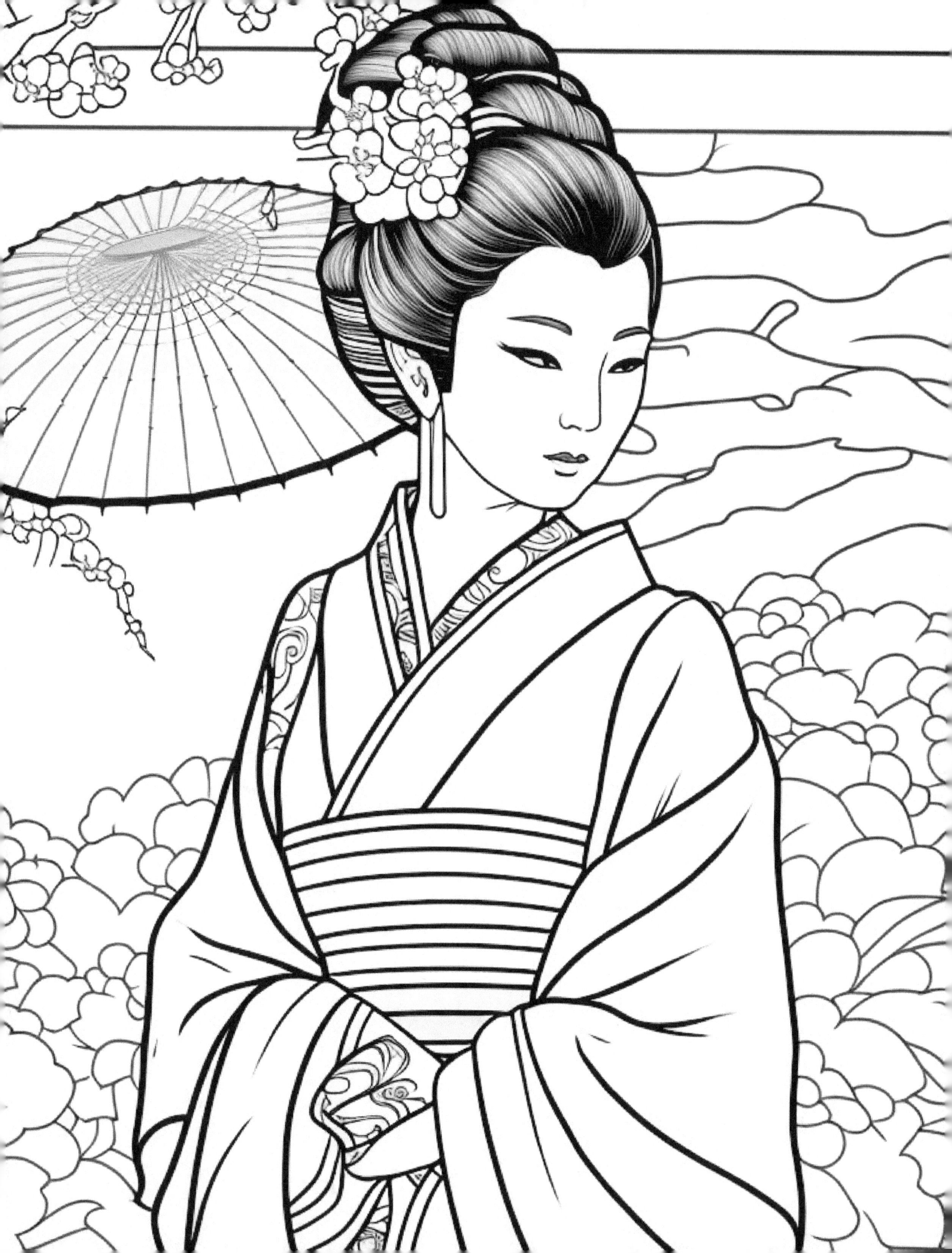

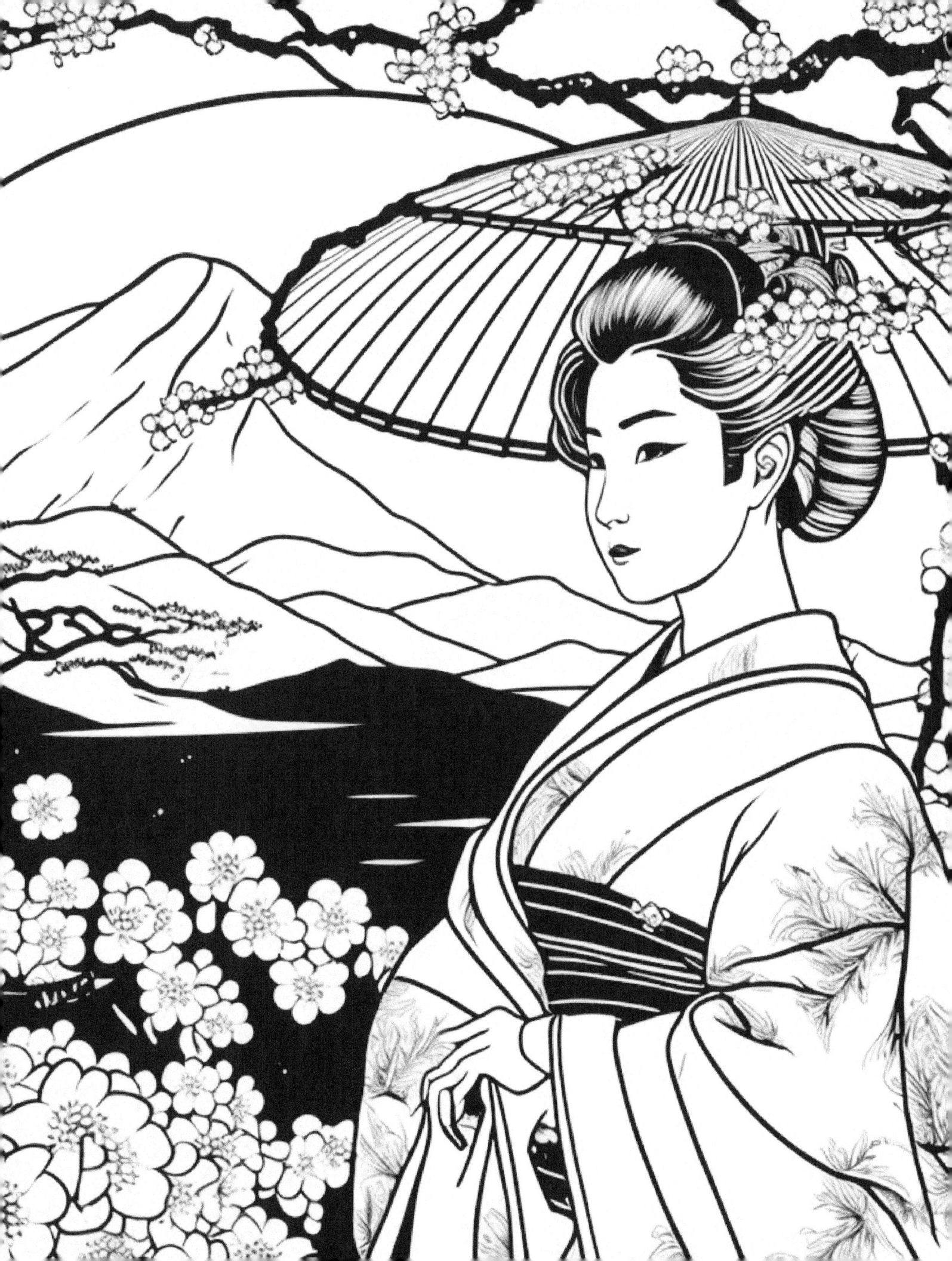

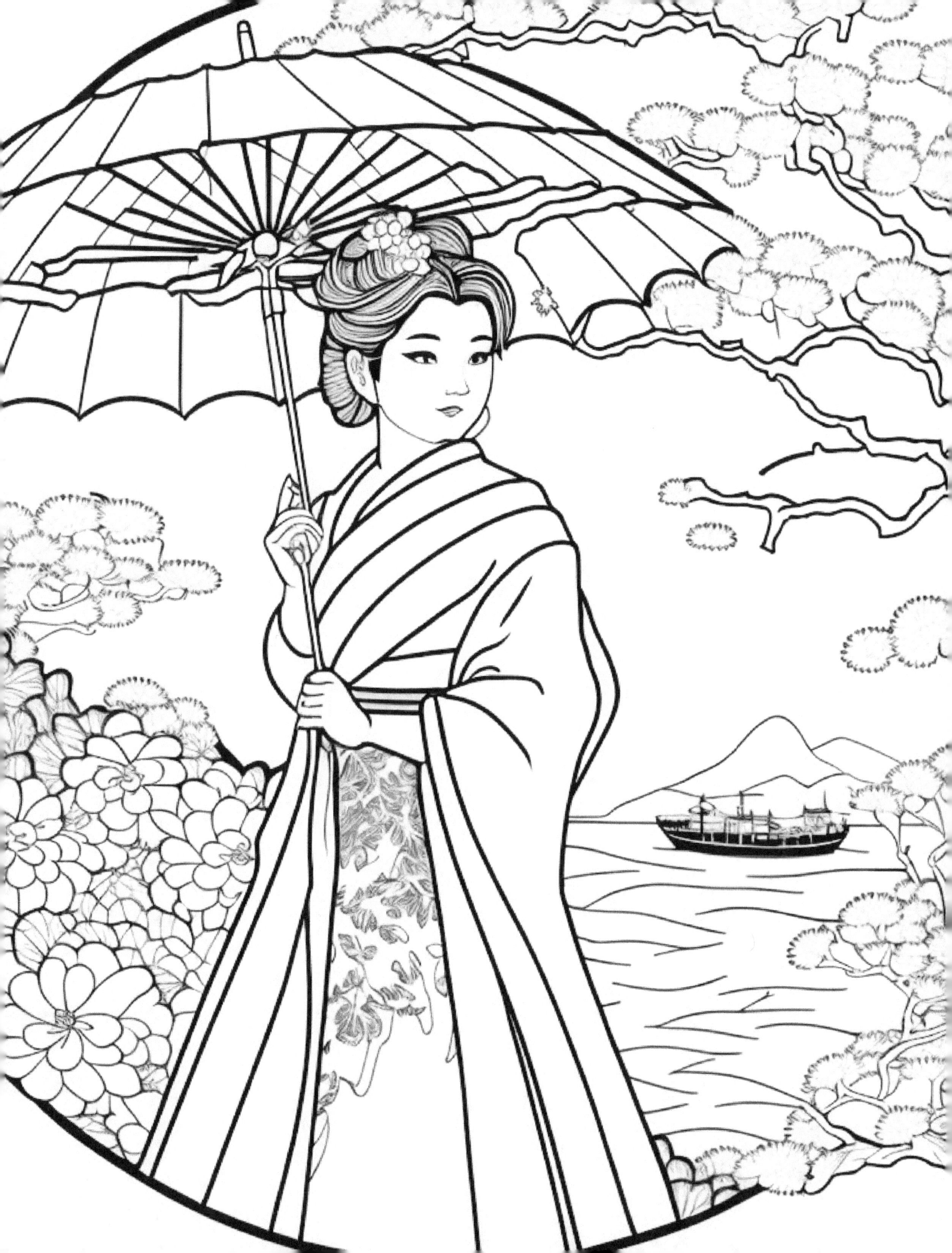

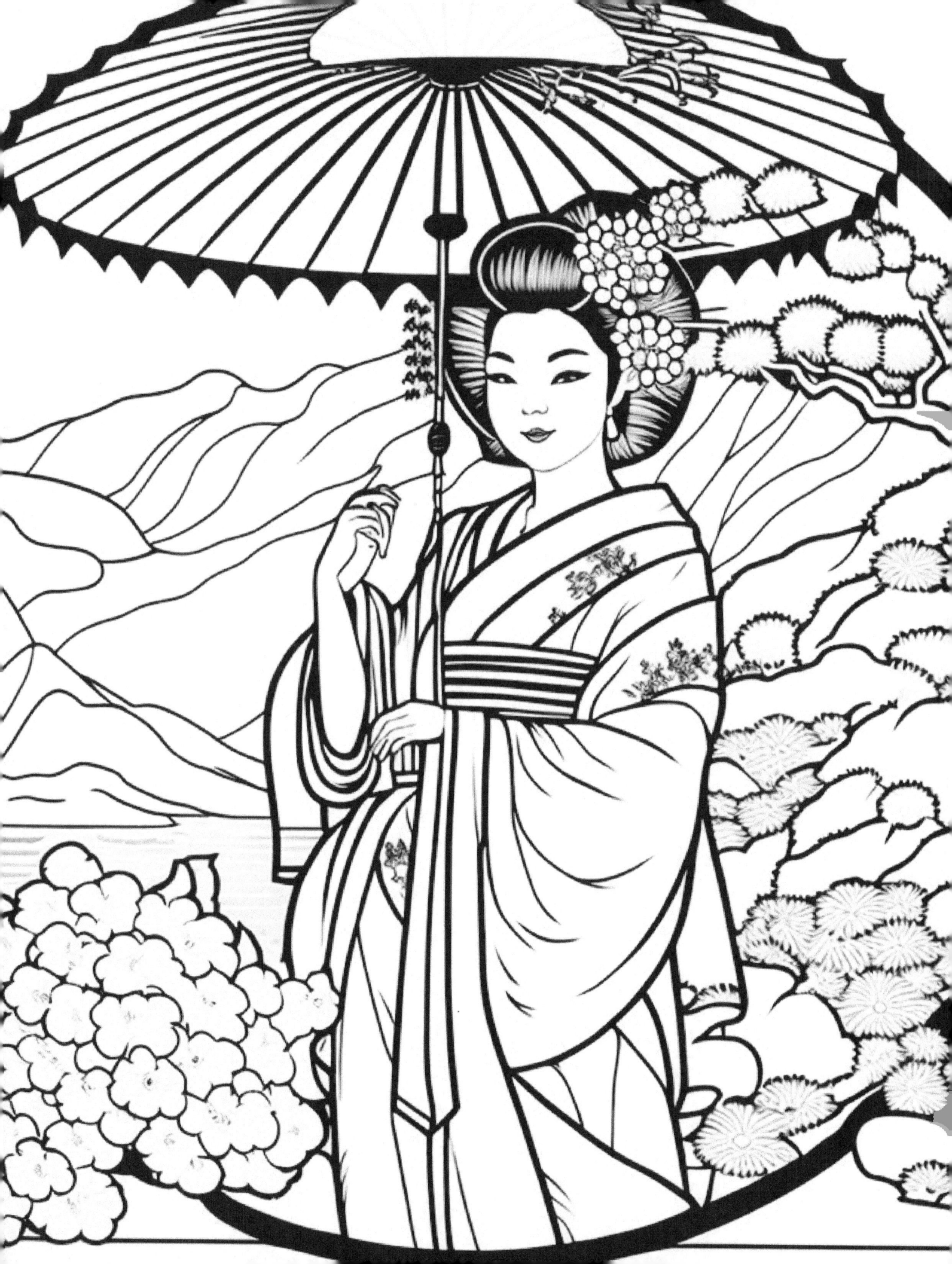

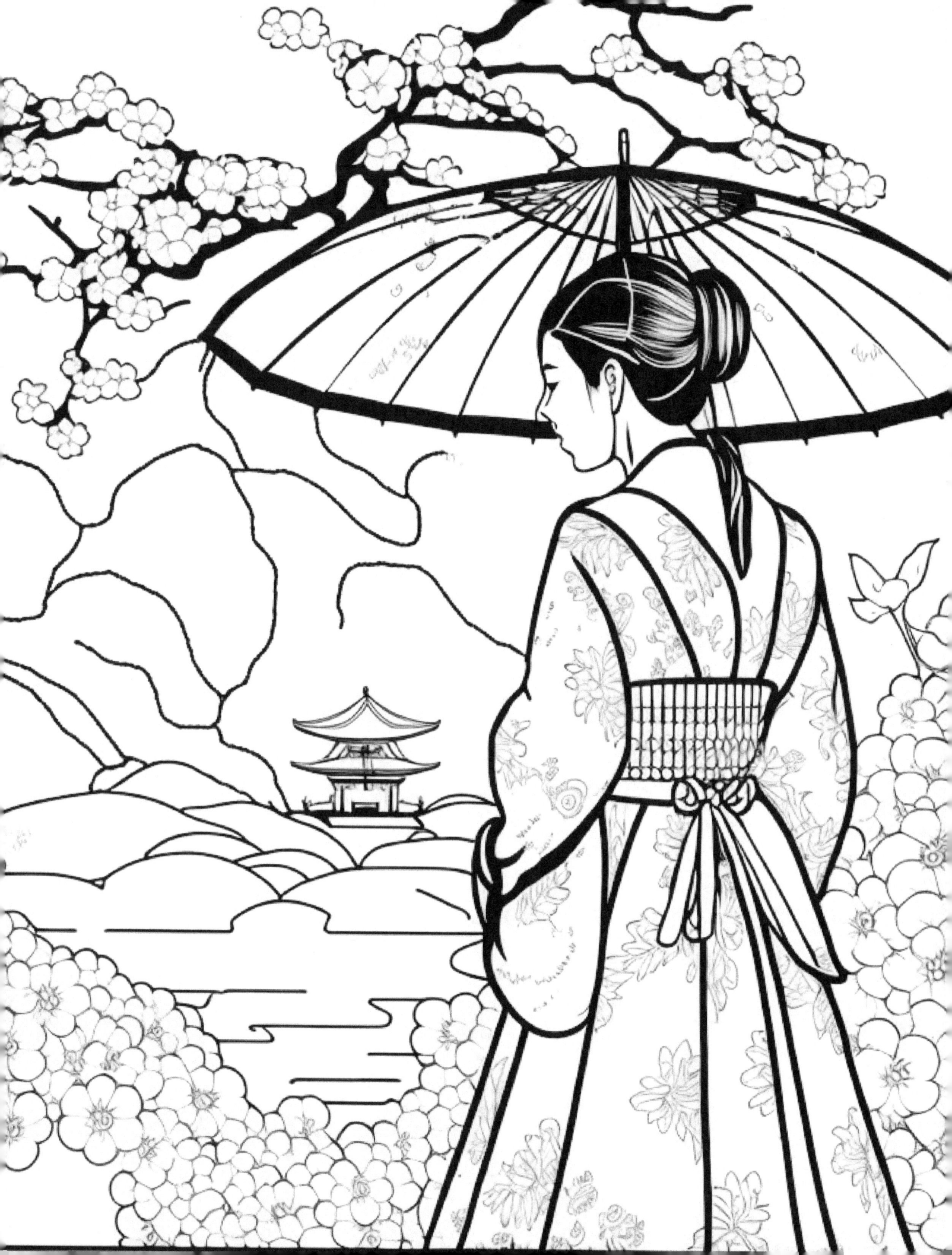

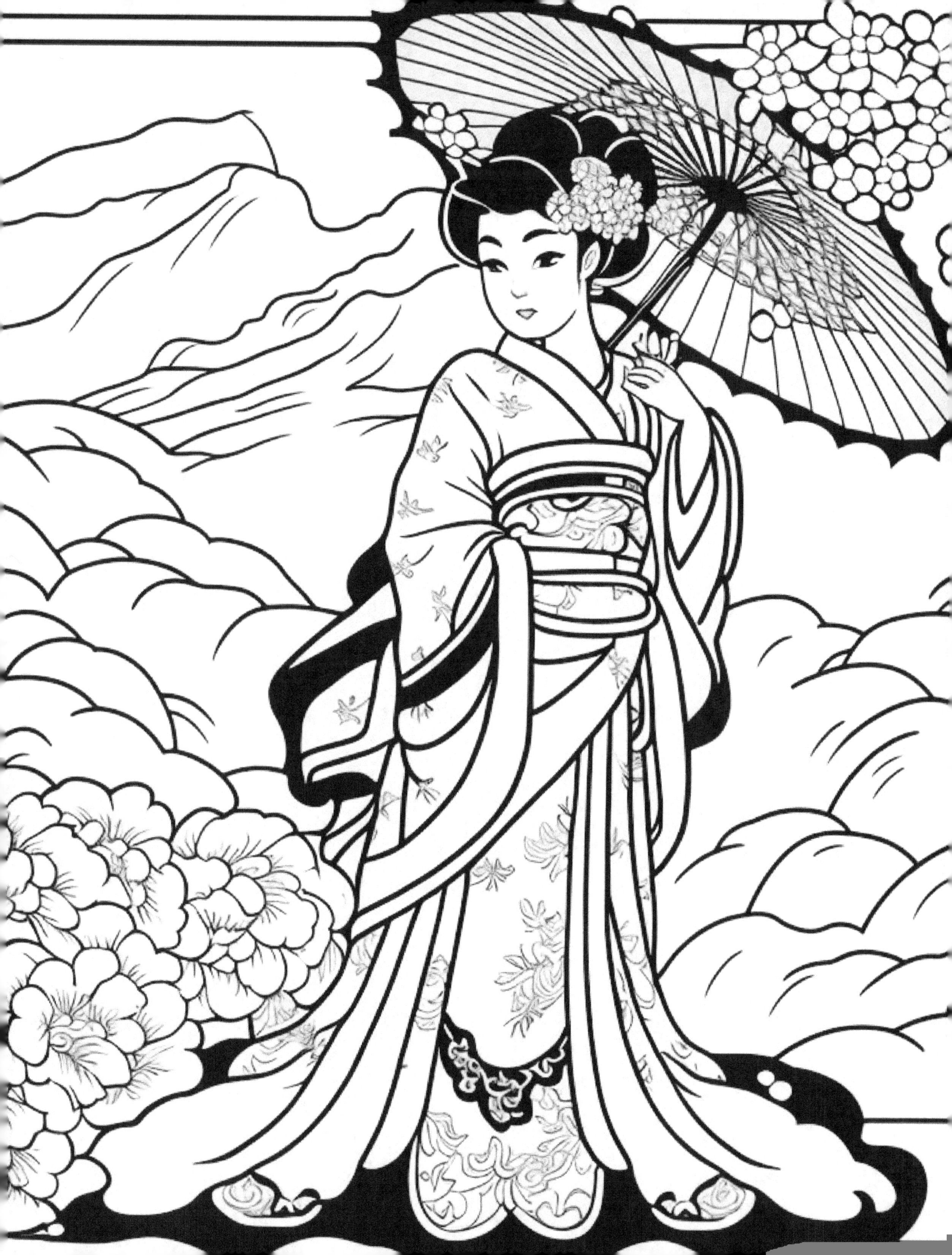

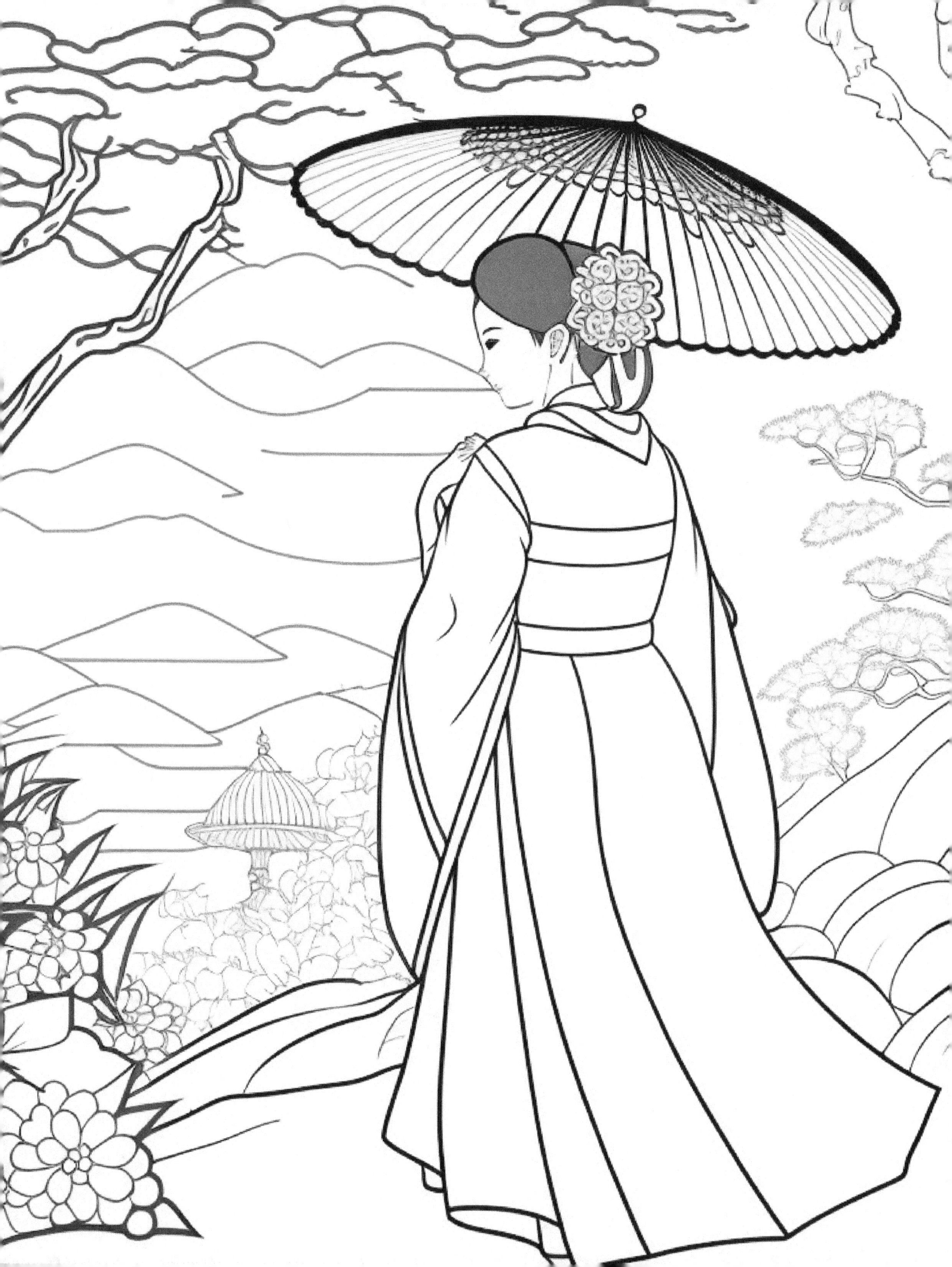

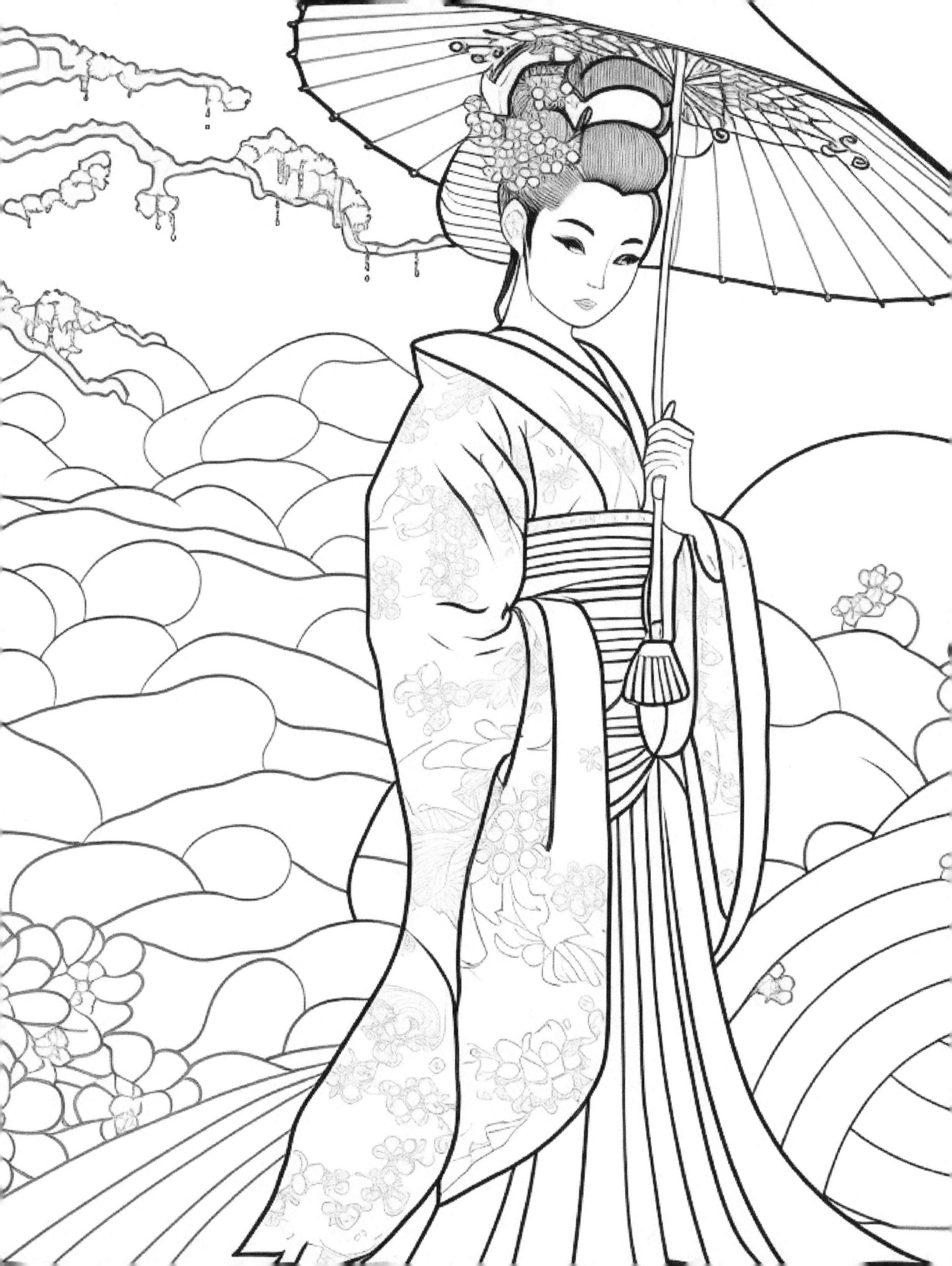

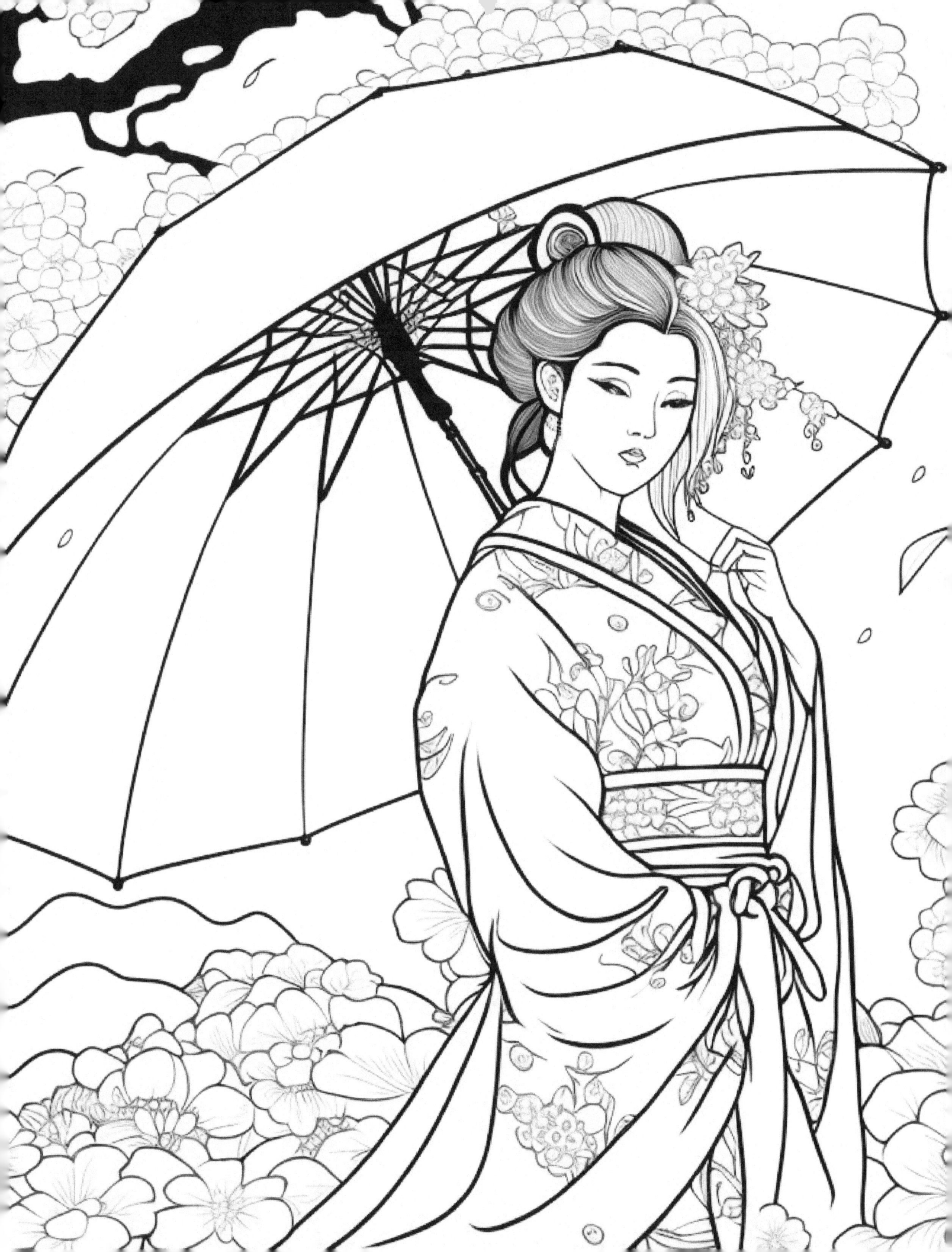

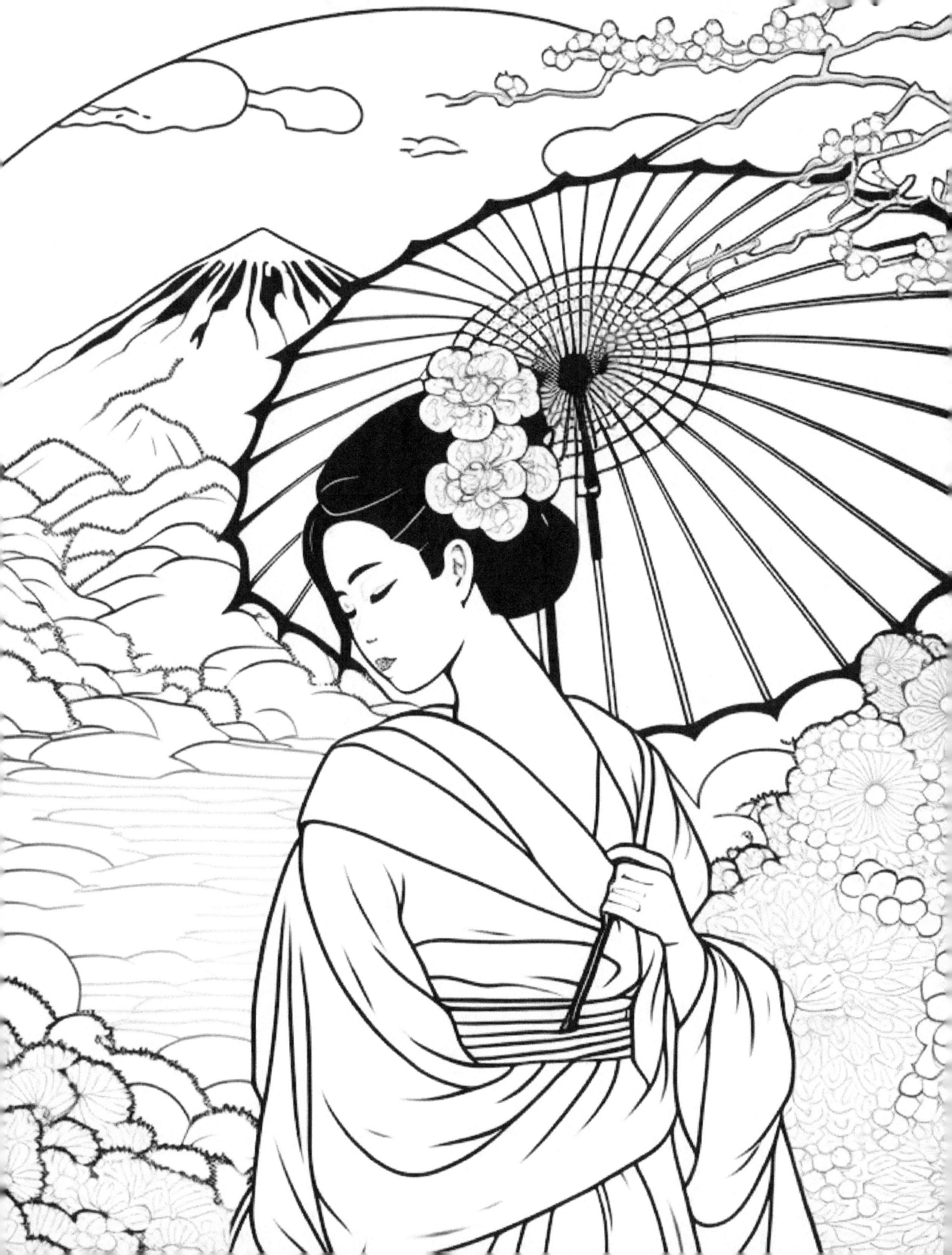

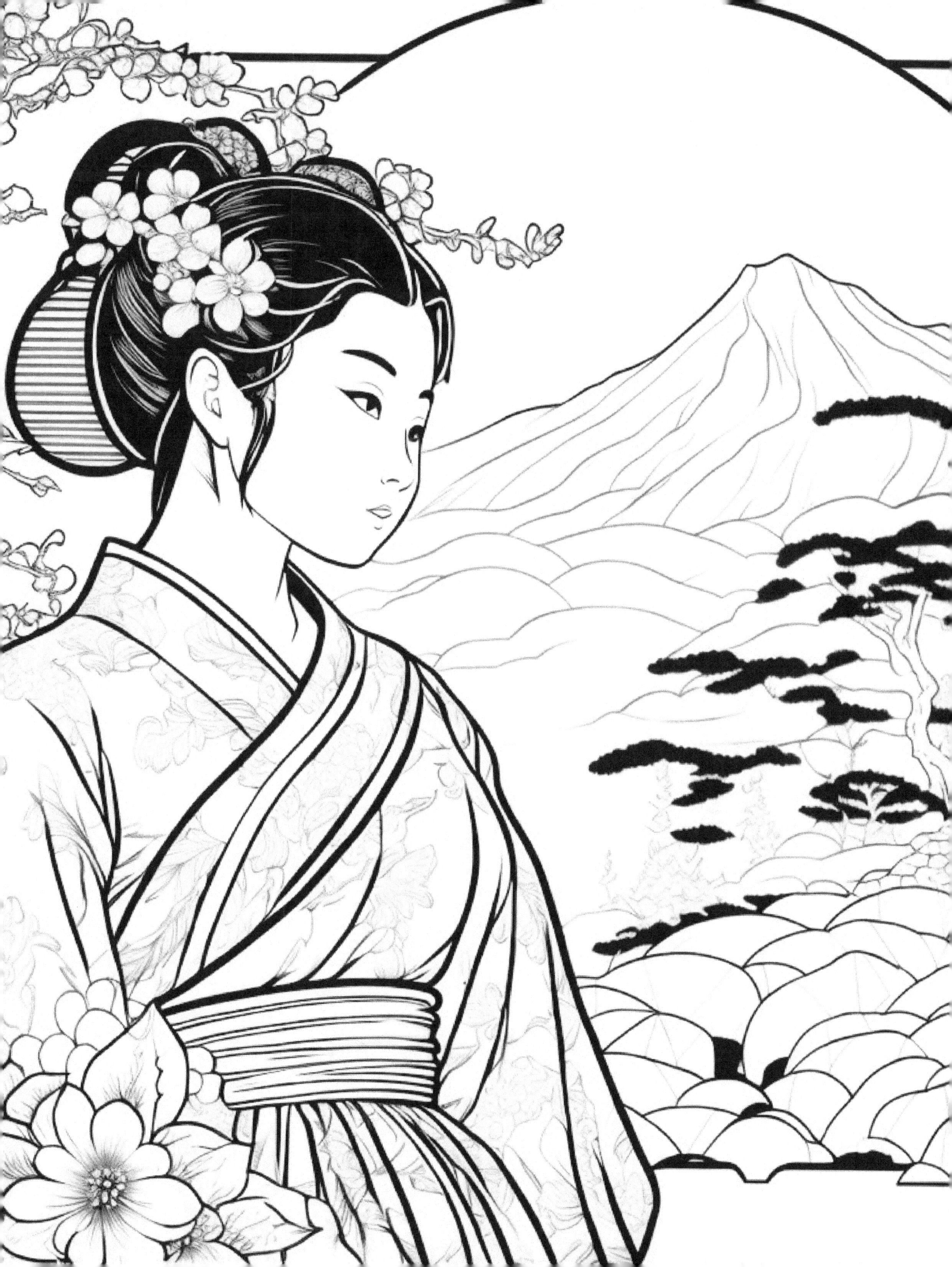

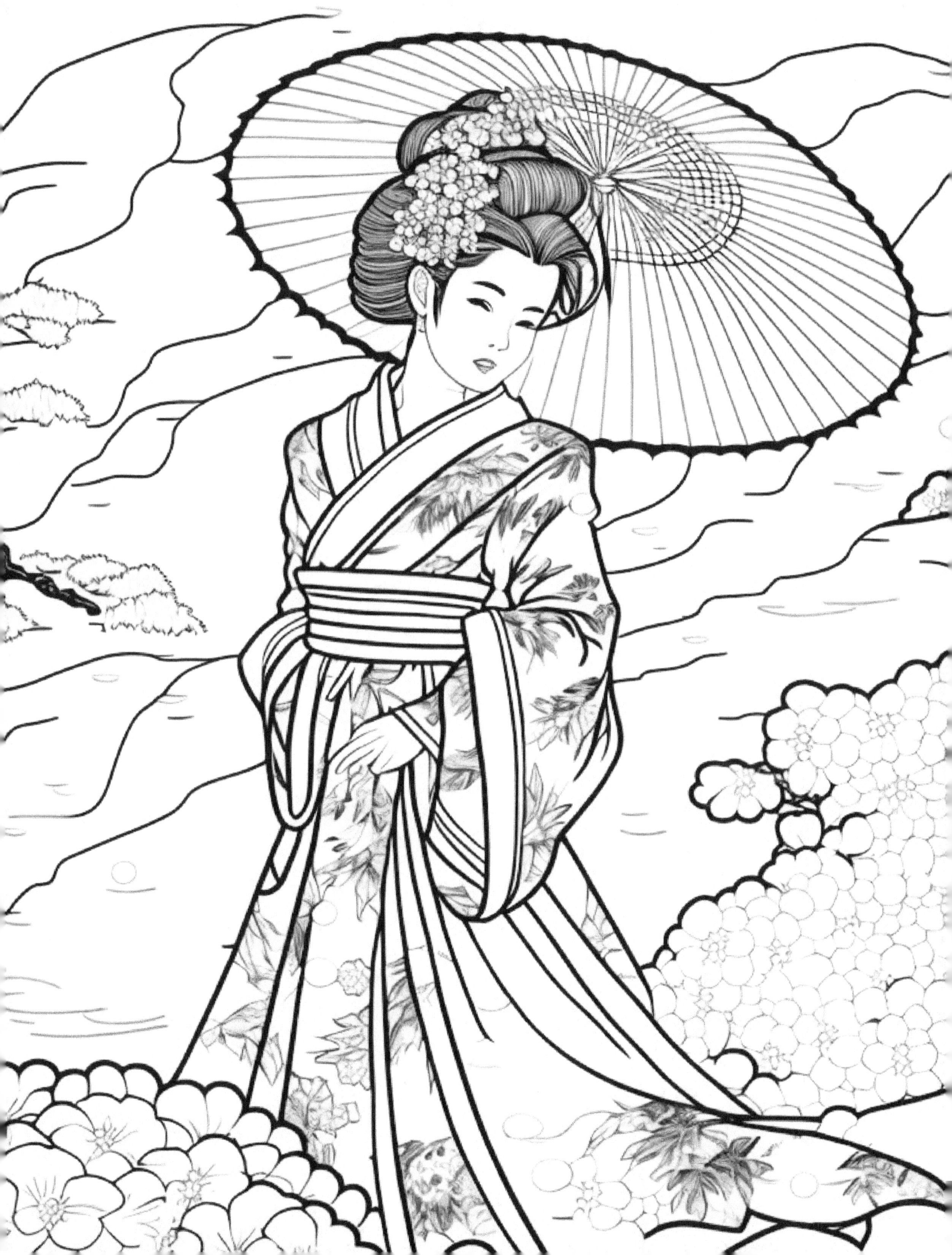

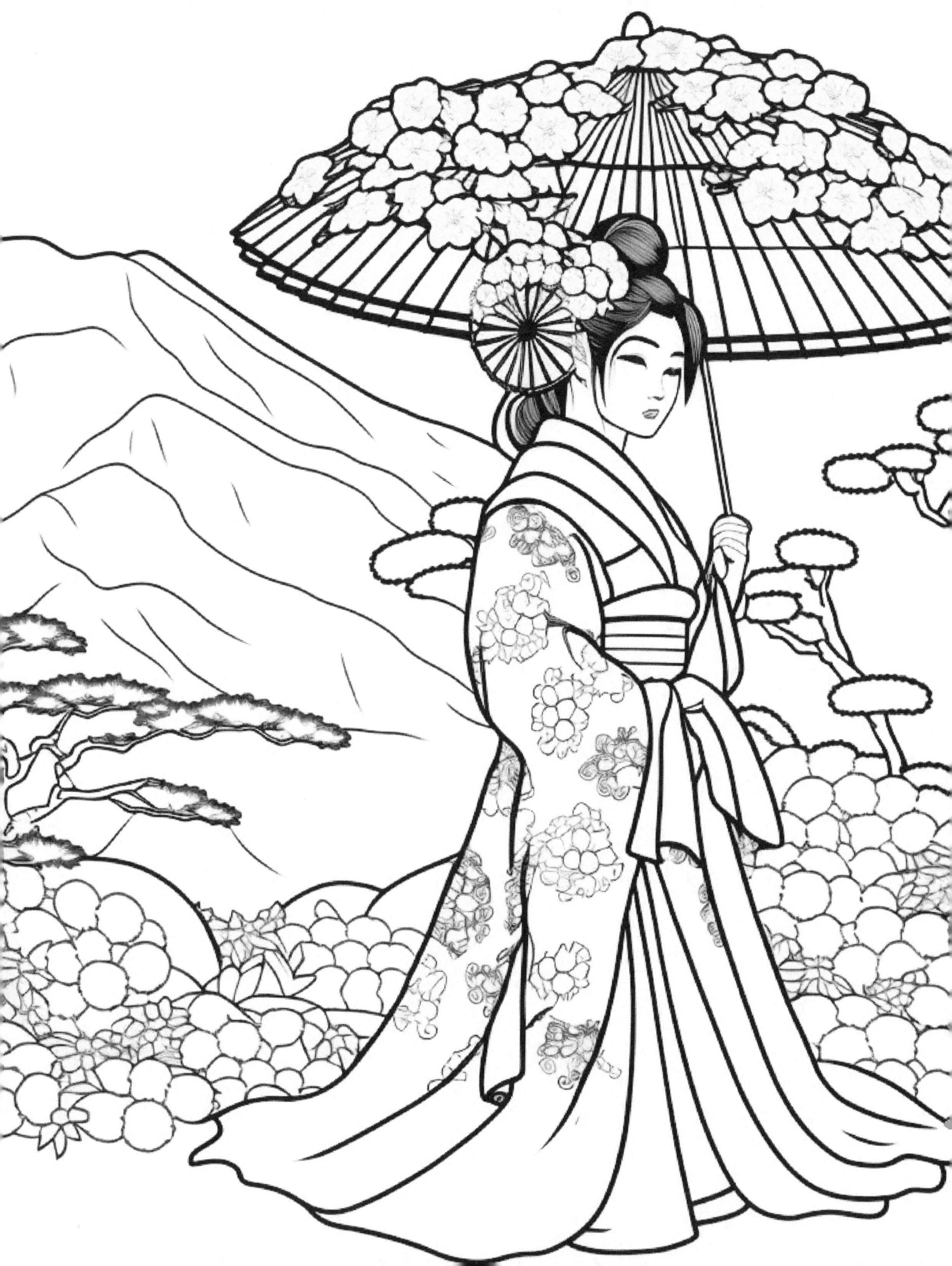

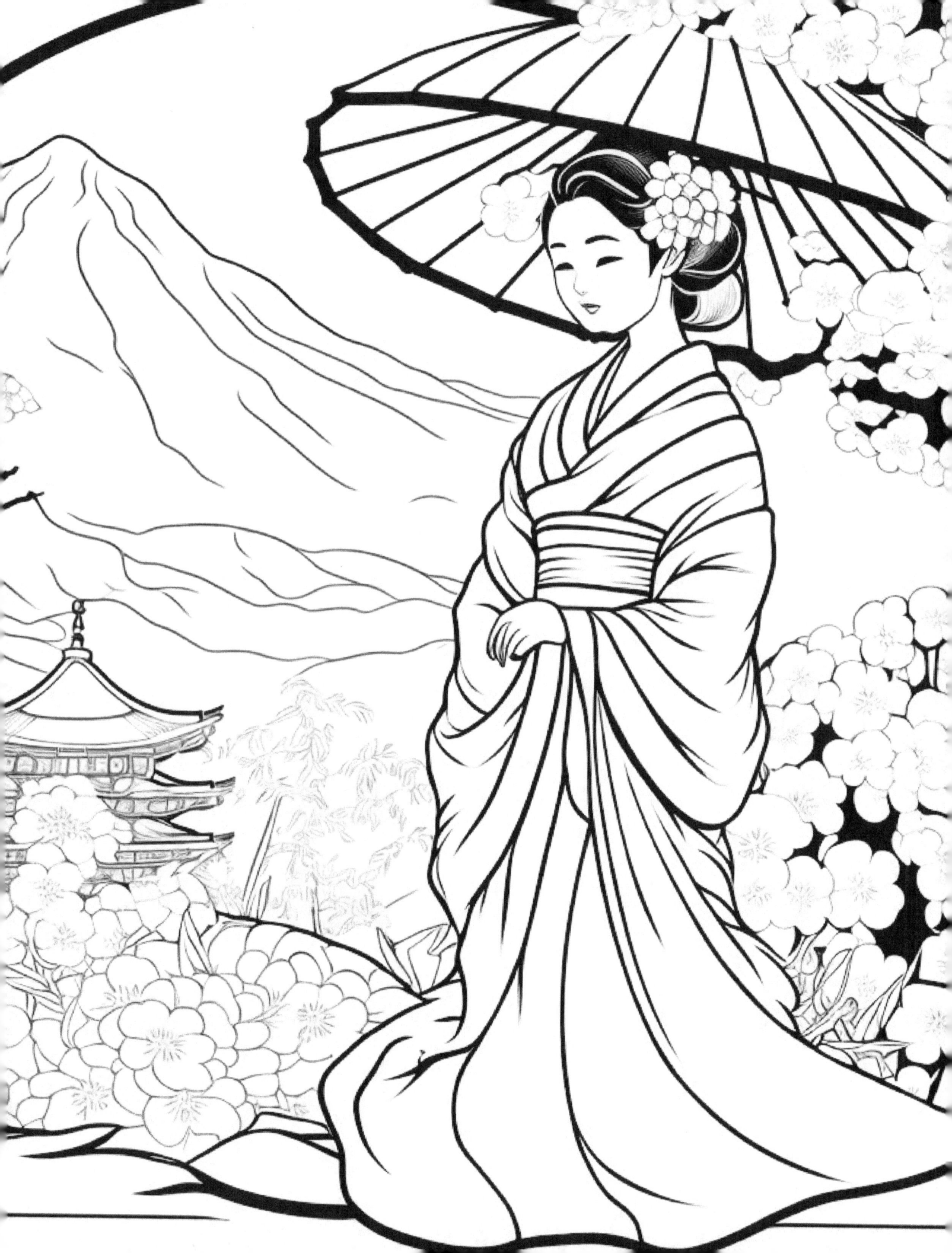

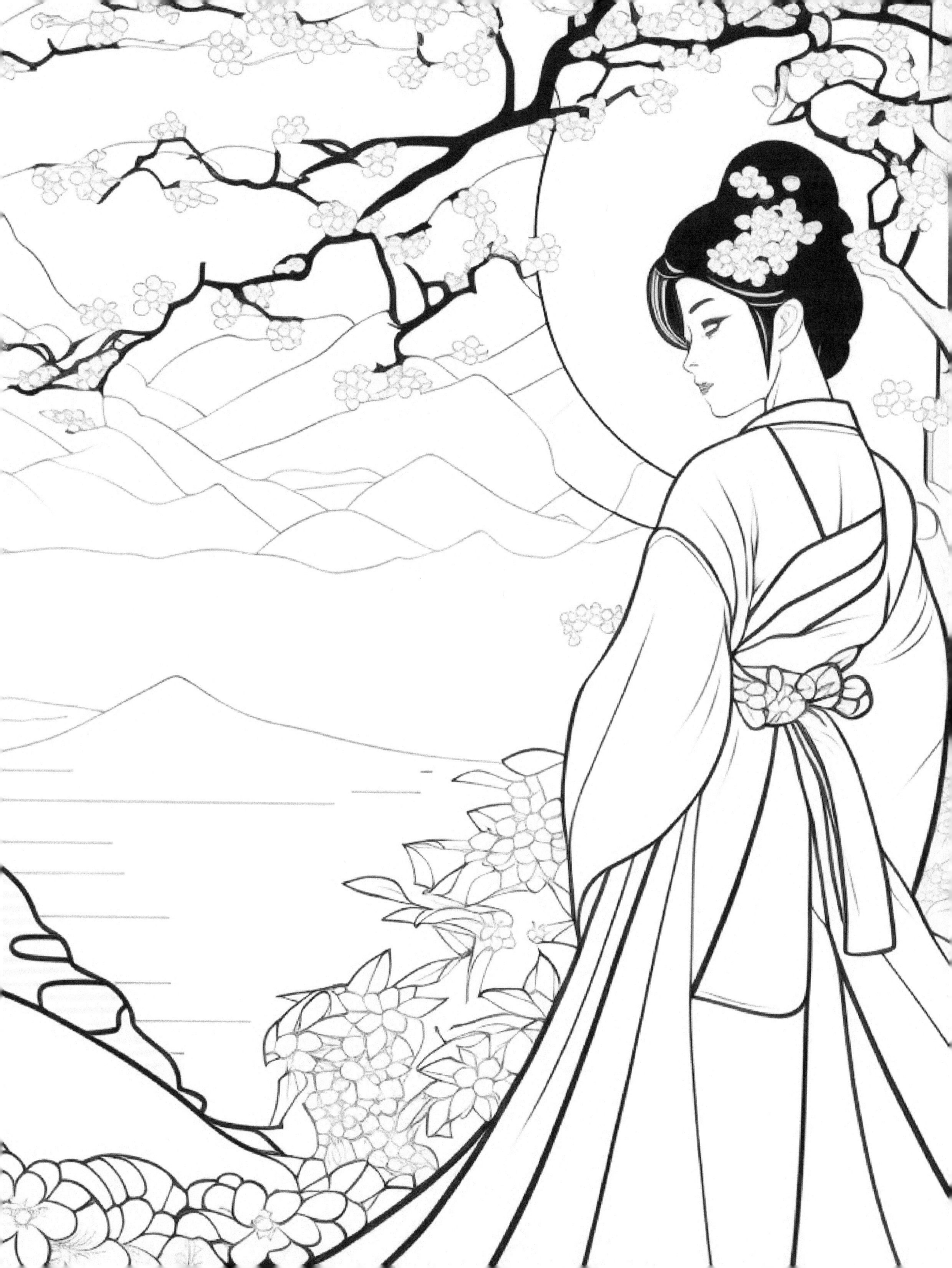

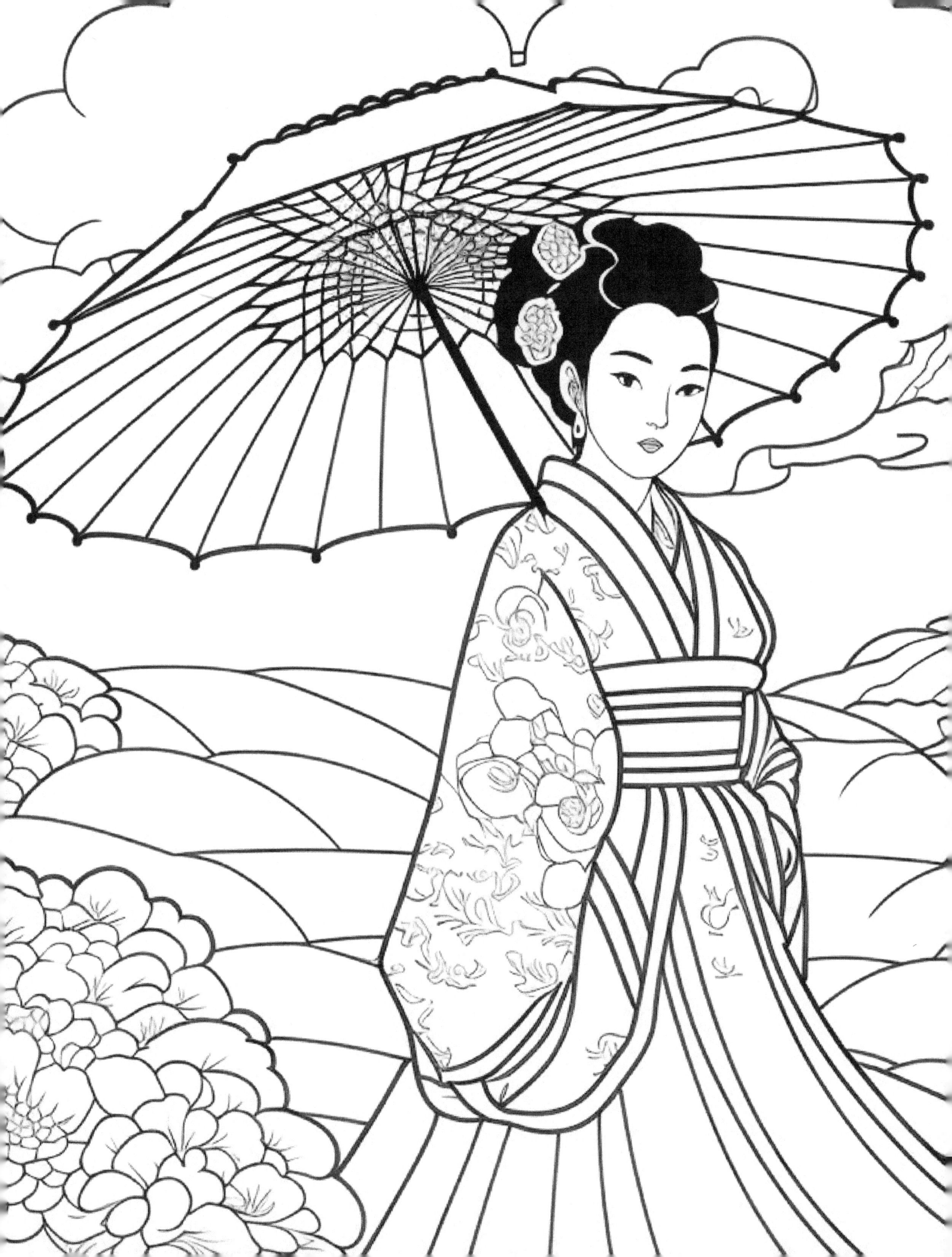

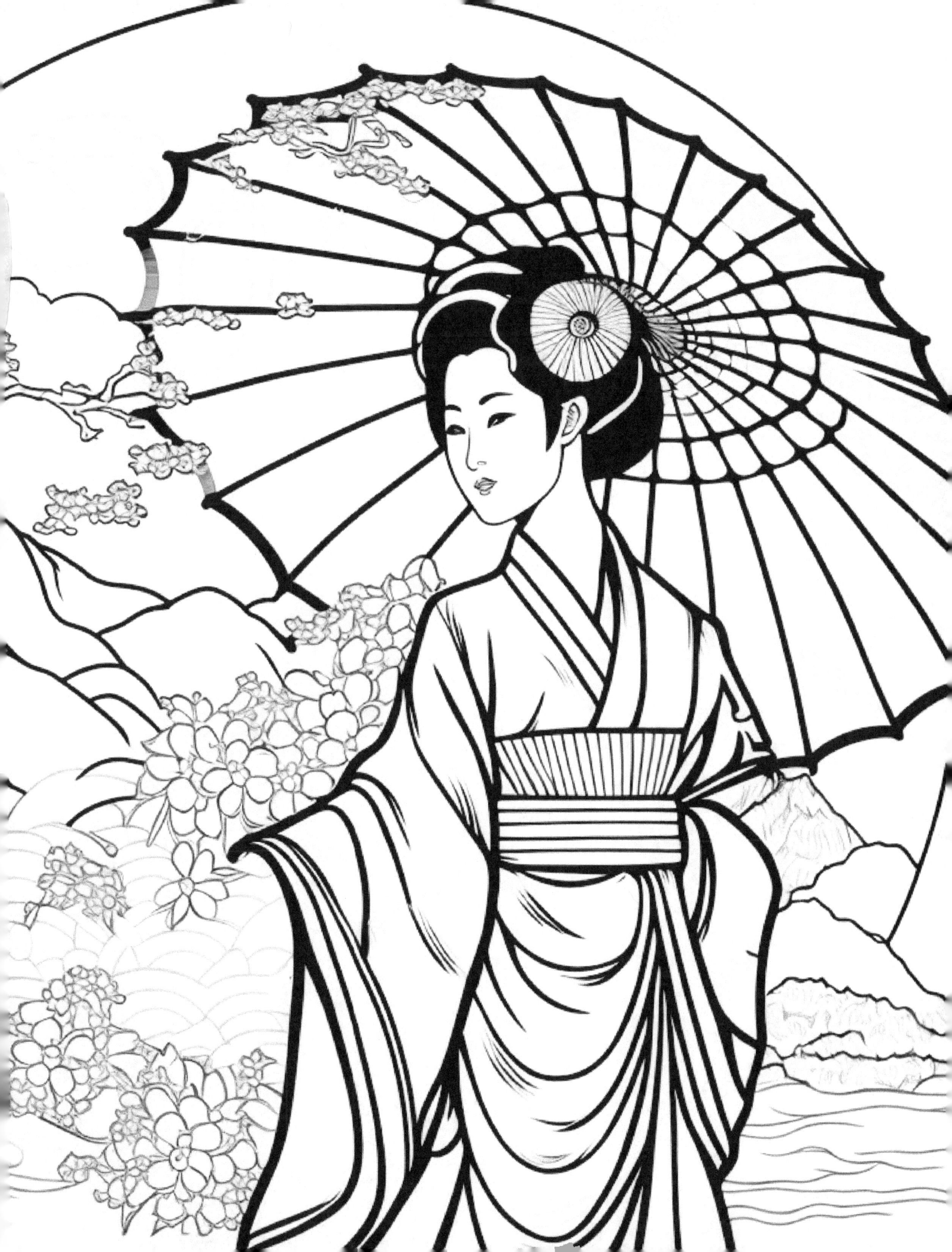

Thank You So Much For Spending Some Time Being Creative With Us.

Please take a look at some of our other activity and coloring books, as well as our large collection of journals.

AH64Designs

www.ingramcontent.com/pod-product-compliance
Lightning Source LLC
Chambersburg PA
CBHW081020240526
45471CB00018B/3916